THE LONG HOME

THE LONG HOME

CHRISTIAN WIMAN

COPPER CANYON PRESS

Cover art: Paul Hunter, *Dry Landscape #AM*, 2006. Gold, copper and acrylic on canvas, 36 x 48 inches. Courtesy of Byron Roche Gallery, Chicago.

Copper Canyon Press is in residence at Fort Worden State Park in Port Townsend, Washington, under the auspices of Centrum. Centrum is a gathering place for artists and creative thinkers from around the world, students of all ages and backgrounds, and audiences seeking extraordinary cultural enrichment.

The Long Home was originally published by Story Line Press, 1998.
Interior design: Paul Joseph Pope

LIBRARY OF CONGRESS CATALOGING-IN-PUBLICATION DATA
Wiman, Christian, 1966–
   The Long home / Christian Wiman.
      p. cm.
   ISBN 978-1-55659-269-0 (alk. paper)
   1. Texas, West—Poetry. I. Title.

PS3573.I47843L66 2008
811'.54—dc22

2007030514

COPPER CANYON PRESS
Post Office Box 271
Port Townsend, Washington 98368
www.coppercanyonpress.org

Acknowledgments

Grateful acknowledgments are made to the following magazines in which some of these poems first appeared:

Kentucky Poetry Review: "Afterwards"; *Passages North*: "Storm Cellar"; *Poet & Critic*: "Fisherman," "Hearing Loss"; *Poetry*: "Elsewhere," "Living Room," "The Long Home (Part V)"; *Sewanee Review*: "Clearing," "Revenant"; *Shenandoah*: "Sweet Dreams," "The Long Home (Part III)"; *The Plum Review*: "The Long Home (Part I)"; *The Threepenny Review*: "One Good Eye"; *TriQuarterly*: "The Long Home (Part II)."

I would also like to thank Stanford University, The University of Texas at Austin and the Texas Institute of Letters, Ruth Lilly and the Modern Poetry Association, the Mary Roberts Rinehart Foundation, and Lynchburg College in Virginia for their support.

Contents

Part I

Part II

Part I

Revenant

She loved the fevered air, the green delirium
in the leaves as a late wind whipped and quickened —
a storm cloud glut with color like a plum.
Nothing could keep her from the fields then,
from waiting braced alone in the breaking heat
while lightning flared and disappeared around her,
thunder rattling the windows. I remember
the stories I heard my relatives repeat
of how spirits spoke through her clearest words,
her sudden eloquent confusion, trapped eyes,
the storms she loved because they were not hers:
her white face under the unburdening skies
upturned to feel the burn that never came:
that furious insight and the end of pain.

Hearing Loss

Only the most obvious questions
were asked her, how she felt
or if she'd slept, and even these words,
before they reached her, wavered free of meanings
as if a wind were in them. Friends and family
came close and called to her
as they would call down a well, peering
into some darkness their own altered voices
might rise out of. In time,
even the echoes faded, until
any moment's simple music —
a bird singing, her grandchildren laughing —
faltered before her, trembling
somewhere in the very air she breathed.
She felt sounds she was hardly conscious of
before: the deep-freezer's door hummed
when touched, and the dry heartbeat
of an old clock ticked lightly into her fingers.
Her son, old himself, would lean over her
trying to make her understand an hour
was all he could stay, it was Sunday
or Monday, or a particular silence
was the silence of rain,
and on the long drive out here
the wet road whispered him home.
                              Waking alone,

dawns so quiet she hears
leaves breathing light, or drifting
alone through days unchanging as smooth water,
she can almost believe the life she remembers
is life. Lovers on the television screen
know only the words she gives them, birds
in the trees sing her memories
of their song. She answers the softest knocks
at her door, surprised each time
that no one is there, she listens intently
to mirrors, stands at a window
bringing the wind inside. Until,
in the muted light of late afternoon
she lies resting, resisting
sleep like a small child
who has stayed up too long, who half dreams
the arms that hold her, the room full of voices
and laughter, but cannot bring herself wholly
into the world where they are.

In Lakeview Cemetery

This is the time of year
the lengthening dark appears
as light in all the trees.

Enameled chestnuts ease
from their skins
and I am holding again

the deep-casked color and shape
a low note might take
before becoming its sound.

Today the rain came down
in clean, elliptical lines
through sunlight, a sign

of something, I remembered,
as the brief shower ended
and the sky cleared.

Now, as I walk here
in the rain-scented air
I hear the sound of water

in the windy trees.
How can I learn to grieve?
The damp shadows of leaves

are printed on stones,
on sidewalks where leaves have blown,
fallen and actual, gone.

Callings

1. *Living Room*

I've heard him coughing hard since four.
Sometime later, he's pulled his chair
across the floor to sit and watch
the sunrise, a half-full cup of pitch-
thick coffee steadied on his thigh.
He doesn't say the light is gathering
in the eyes of children not yet born,
that dawn's the time to call the Lord,
so pray, child, before the whole world
wants to. In the space he makes
for me against his chest I drift away
for what seem like years to me. I wake
into the life another day brings
and the heartbeat in my ears is deafening.

2. Storm Cellar

Sundust. Buried air.
Jars of darkness
on the shelves, preserves
with taped-on names
and dates I am
just learning to read;
tools, flashlights
and blankets for the storm
that's not yet come,
one wall showing dim
and root-veined
like a stilled lung.
I no longer hear,
from my hiding
place, faint
as though from far
away, my name:
my grandfather, mingled
with the wind, pretending
to wonder where I've gone.
He is quiet now,
flickering in and out
of the door, a shadow
alive in the light,
waiting for me to give
in, for some sound
to escape me.

Clearing

It was when I walked lost
in the burn and rust
of late October that I turned
near dusk toward the leaf-screened
light of a green clearing in the trees.
In the untracked and roadless open
I saw an intact but wide open house,
half-standing and half-lost
to unsuffered seasons of wind
and frost: warped tin and broken stone,
old wood combed by the incurious sun.
The broad wall to the stark north,
each caulked chink and the solid hearth
dark with all the unremembered fires
that in the long nights quietly died,
implied a life of bare solitude
and hardship, little to hold
and less to keep, aching days
and welcome sleep in the mind-clearing cold.
And yet the wide sky, the wildflowered ground
and the sound of the wind
in the burn and rust of late October
as the days shortened and the leaves turned
must have been heartening, too,
to one who walked out of the trees
into a green clearing that he knew.
If you could find this place,

or even for one moment feel
in the word-riddled remnants
of what I felt there
the mild but gathering air, see the leaves
that with one good blast would go,
you could believe
that standing in a late weave of light and shade
a man could suddenly want his life,
feel it blaze in him and mean,
as for a moment I believed,
before I walked on.

What I Know

These fields go farther than you think they do.
That darkness is my father walking away.
It is my shadow that I tell this to.

This stillness is not real. The cloud that grew
Into an old man's face didn't stay.
These fields go farther than you think they do.

The sun loves shattered things, and loves what's new.
I love you so much more than I can say.
It is my shadow that I tell this to.

He is not sleeping, that bird the bugs crawl through.
Don't touch. Don't cry. Think good things. Pray.
These fields go farther than you think they do.

Some darknesses breathe, look back at you.
Under the porch a pair of eyes waits all day.
It is my shadow that I tell this to.

The things my father told me must be true:
There are some places where you cannot play.
These fields go farther than you think they do.
It is my shadow that I tell this to.

Afterwards

...it is no great distance
From slimness to cool water.
—Ovid

There is nothing left for anyone to hold.
The days are long and mild, and parts
of herself are drifting imperceptibly
into them. She almost remembers rain,
each drop colder than she is, clearer.
Her face becomes the face of everyone
who looks into her, her longings their own.
When she feels the warm bodies of children
swimming inside of her, or lovers
under the shadows on her skin,
she wants to carry them all down
into her deepest reaches. They leave
silvered with tears. On clear nights she wears
the moon like a soft jewel and dreams
of a world as still and silent as she is.
The least touch leaves her whole body trembling.

Sweet Dreams

Voices fade as he walks
into them. He hears his name
in the air above him, passed
from parents to guests
and back to him like a ball.
The plates have faces. In his
father's he sees his own.
The candle's shadow is talking
and laughing with the wall.
There are kind questions
for him, shared silences he hears
himself speak into: he blinks,
whispers to the floor,
a small fist blooms with years
he's stored in fingers. Somewhere
in their watches are the hours
he can't enter. In awkward
pauses some stare into his sleep.
A red-nailed finger slowly circles
the rim of a glass, but the red
bell of wine won't sing.
They look at him and smile.
His mother stands, her hand enclosing
his. His father's cheek cuts
into his kiss. The hardwood floor
shines eyes of light. The dark
doorway is the wall's yawn.
He walks into their wishes.

One Good Eye

Lost in the lush flesh
of my crannied aunt,
I felt her smell
of glycerine, rosewater
and long enclosure
enclosing me,
and held my breath
until she'd clucked
and muttered me
to my reluctant
unmuttering uncle
within whose huge
and pudgy palm
my own small-boned hand
was gravely taken,
shaken, and released.
Sunday: sunlight
oozing through drawn blinds
of the dining room
over fried okra
and steaming greens,
cherry yum-yum
and candied yams,
Navy knives and forks,
placemats picturing
national parks.
Bless these gifts
we're about to receive,

my uncle mumbled
and my aunt amened,
before with slow clinks
and shakes, amphibious
slurps and gurgles,
they dug untasting
in, bits of gifts
not quite received
tumbling down
laminated canyons,
improbable waterfalls,
far, clear mountains.
Nothing stopped
unless I stopped:
their mouths surprised
wide on half-finished
mouthfuls, my aunt
in unfeigned alarm
straining a full bowl
or meat-laden plate
in front of me,
little jiggles
shooting through
wattled, weighted
arms and my iced tea.
Exhausted, sprawled
on vinyl recliners
in the dim glooms
of the half-lit den,
they shouted down
the loud television

telling me
which neighbor's name
was in the news
that week, whose heart
stopped in sleep,
or some man by cancer
eaten clean away.
It's early yet,
they'd sigh and say
if I sighed or said
anything at all
about leaving,
nodding their heads
at me and nodding
noisily off
like a parody
of people sleeping:
my aunt's face crazed
with whiskery twitches,
her glass eye slitted
eerily open;
the unmuscled melt
of my uncle,
broad-skulled, flaring
forested nostrils.
The lamp, handcrafted
out of Coke cans,
flickered erratically
if I moved. The clock,
shaped like the state —
El Paso nine,

Amarillo noon,
and the vast plastic
where we were — ticked
each itchy instant.
Then it was time:
my uncle blundering
above me, gasping
tobacco and last
enticements;
— while my aunt,
bleary, tears bright
in her one good eye,
fussed and wished
the day was longer,
kissed and sloshed
herself around me,
a long last hold
from which I held
myself back,
enduring each
hot, wet breath, each
laborious beat
of her heart, thinking
it would never end.

Fisherman

In the end, when he was laid out
speechless and vanishing and made
no wants known but light, friends brought food
and took turns telling his stories
back to him.
              He was four years old
and couldn't let go, soaked and scared
to be in the river with what-
ever had pulled him there. Laughter
seeped through the walls of his childhood
as he drifted asleep, his father's
voice heard from some near room, rising
in the darkness around his bed.

As the voice became his own, his
room became the sea. Half-drunk, giddy
with his good fortune, he cast out
again with his wife, honeymooning,
both flicking in blues without bait.
In the silent space between two
waves she touched him.
                  Storming in
from a storm, he was twenty years
younger, thirty years younger,
slickered and shaking a string
of fish before their wide unblinking
eyes, or filling his empty hands
with the fighting, tremendous fish

that struck every time in the dark
pools of their minds, then broke free again
in the telling.
                    Drawn to him
once more, all too old for fishing
but each glad to have this one chance
to come together, they outdid
each other for days with catches
from the past. Coming close they'd tell
themselves that he'd smiled or they'd seen
him move, that they'd all fish again,
that he would hold on forever.

Elsewhere

All he remembers is a whisper
high in the trees,
a breeze out of nowhere
he walks with, for there was no one
where he was.
There are lulls
and shiftings, eddies
in the air, inflections
so slight he thinks,
as he sways and changes,
he chooses them. Home
is momentary, a way
of seeing, a sweet lingering
in a cloud before it drifts
beyond the form he's found
for it, a brief
impalpable life breathed
into clothes on a line.
Restless, attuned
to wayward fluencies,
he craves the space
of fields, learns to lose
himself amid the haphazard
songs of abandoned
houses, empty wells
and the hollows of bones,
quickening, assenting
to the distances

into which he is
borne. The world begins to blur
around him, landscapes altering
as he enters them: revisions,
erosions, clouds
flowing like smoke over.
In time, he seems less
moved than a part
of that which once moved him,
his presence only a passing
havoc in what he's touched:
leaves scattered
and lost, bodies of dust
swirling. He longs
to find some calm within
what he's become, inside
the sound, a roaming
stillness. It seems
so close, as if he might,
even now, blink and be
there, restored, prepared,
whispering all he remembers.

Part II

The Long Home

...because man goeth to his long home,
and the mourners go about the streets.

O Lord, honey, I can remember pretty far back,
but I don't know nothin' 'bout what it is I remember.

I

We drove all day on roads without a speck
Of paving, not knowing but knowing not
To ask when we would stop or where. Papa
Let no one drive but him. The rest of us —
Mama, Grandma and Grandpa, Cole, M.A.,
Joseph, Sister and me — wove into the warm
Tune of air whistling through our open windows
Words that would be our lives when we arrived
At Papa's dream. *We'll have our own farm,*
A great big passel of cattle. We'll grow
Cotton as big as fists, as white as cream,
And we'll be rich as kings when we come home.
Across the Texas line the land was curved
And deep green like Carolina. Elms
And old oaks grew. A willow swayed so slow
When we went by it seemed submerged in water.

I remember that. And I remember seeing,
Past Abilene, the sun come plunging down
In front of us and spatter back in the sky.
It was like no sunset we'd ever seen.
Thick light dripped and puddled on the far
Horizon, yellow smeared and flecked with red
Like a broken yolk that had begun
To grow. There was a moment when the sky,
Ground, and the air between were all one color,
My family's faces, too, glowing, fading ...
Then everything was gone and we were driving
In the darkness toward whatever edge the day
Had fallen from, whatever space it now
Was falling into.
              There were hardly trees
At all: mesquites all gnarled and swiveled up
With wind, a solitary cottonwood
Reaching out of the long and level ground
Like a plea. We would drive an hour out here
Without a change in landscape telling us
The time was gone, the sky a mild blue curve
Above, touching the ground on every side
As if we were within some giant eye.
I felt afraid. All of us did. One dawn,
While everyone still slept, I saw their arms
Across each other and their faces soothed
With dew. A sound was once a part of the dream
It ended: it drew me out into the night,
Into Mama's arms and was her, awake
And crying over us.

It seemed our hold
On earth had weakened. In such space
You might one night wake falling into stars,
Or with a full moon shining from inside
Of you. Working alone, sowing a field
Of light in spring, you might begin to feel
Your shadow is the only shadow in the world;
Or hear in late October wind one day
The whispering hours and distances, soft callings
In a voice so like your own you leave your work
And wander off, wading a level cloud
Of cotton blooming in a blackland farm
As far as you can see.
                              I was ten years old,
The youngest but for Sister, in whose eyes
Words rose up slowly like bits of driftwood
A hand releases underwater. She'd stare
And stare until your name occurred to her,
Suddenly rippling you into the world
With a smile. Sister wasn't right. Before
I married Tom, she'd hardly leave my side.
Chopping cotton, pulling bolls, I'd sing
Or dream out loud, forgetting she was there.
Until she wasn't. Looking around I'd see,
Down in the leaves two rows over, a flicker
Of skin and hair eye-level with an insect.
Or she'd have stopped just ten feet back, her arm
Outstretched, her face completely serious,
Her fist uncurling on a single lock
Of cotton in her palm ... And then her high

Delighted laughter everywhere over me
Like sunlight.
                        We spent a year day-laboring
On farms around Roscoe, our home an old
Abandoned two-room house beside a pump-
Station outside of town, our beds tom-steadies
Built in the walls. Those early nights were warm
And rhythmical, machinery endlessly
In search of oil, a heart of perfect sleep
And unremembered dreams they pulled me from
At dawn. By day, winds blurred the world with tears,
Or stilled completely to unbreathing instants
When I would hear my family's footsteps
And my own, their hands and mine reaching in leaves.
Each morning Mama packed a lunch and stuffed
Our pockets full of fresh-peeled, cloth-soft cornshucks,
Or full of all the things we couldn't own
On ripped-out pages of a catalogue.
Sometime each day we freely gave away
What Papa called the richest, purest fertilizer
This sorry state had ever seen. All day
Six days a week we worked in fields. The boys
Would trade their lunches for an extra hour
Of sleep, or for the half-bag of cotton
They'd come up short the day before. M.A.,
Ignoring Papa's sternest warnings, reeled
Sometimes sundrunk and moaning over the rows
Toward Mama, collapsing like his heart had failed.
But she'd just duck her head and go on picking,
Trying her hardest not to laugh. That year

Even Grandma and Grandpa hardly missed
A day, out there until his face was tanned
And crannied as a peach's pit; and she,
Diminishing within her clothes, all skirt
And empty sleeves, riffled among the rows
Like a living wind. Each evening, outside,
They'd sit and watch the sun go down, saying
That day's pains to the darkness, as the darkness
Gathered them in.
                                We moved ten miles
To Champion, sharecropped the farm that in eight years
We'd own. I started school and spent the whole
First week recalling stories of our trip.
A high, white door appeared and slowly opened.
I stepped inside and drifted through the light
And silence of the house where I was born,
Touched all the furniture we had to leave
Behind, creaked open closets full of clothes.
Reaching beneath my bed, I ran my hand
Over the basketful of riverstones
From which I'd been allowed to bring just one ...
Then someone blinked or spoke that world away
And I was standing in six children's eyes
In Champion, Texas, 1925,
Holding that stone up high for them to see.
I told of how our trailer fell apart
Just forty miles from home because Grandpa
Had built the axle backwards (Papa just sat
Inside the car, shaking his head); of how
I'd stood right up against the ferry's rail

Crossing the Mississippi, daring the ten-
Foot tickle fish that Papa swore would leap
And pluck me down into eternities
Of tickling. And when they asked me why we'd come
At all, I told of how one night in Carolina,
In wind brisking the dying pines and dust
Of our drought-scoured fields, Papa heard clear
And unmistakable the voice of God
And turned and said to Mama suddenly
To hell with it, we'll go to Texas,
A story told so many times it might
By now be ours.

                    There must have been some moment,
At dinner maybe, or all of us together
On the porch, when someone wondered out loud
Again when we'd return, and Papa stopped
Whatever he was doing, shucking shells
Or tearing bread, and looked into his hands
So long that all of us looked down there too.
It must have seemed, for just an instant then,
Like being shaken from a dream, each unsure
Of what the darkness held, or if the world
Our blinking eyes recovered was the same:
Steam rising warm in our amazed faces,
Or evening's shadows edging toward the porch
For all of us, as Papa's hands trembled
Slightly, and Mama breathed out slowly, *Well …*
And we began belonging to this place.

II

A rooster creaked into the silence like
A rusted hinge, as if each dawn a door
Swung slowly open into light.
I'd be outside before the moon burned away,
Sleepwalking through my morning chores, the fields
And few mesquite trees silvering into sight,
Cattle clumped on the ground like breathing stones.
I'd help the boys haul slop, carry kindling,
Or drift alone into the henhouse, testing
Stillness as you might walk on water skimmed
With ice, easing my hands beneath each hen
To steal her heat before I stole her eggs ...
Until M.A. or Papa slapped the walls
Outside and laughed as all around me birds
Exploded into sound. In the afternoons
When school was out, we'd work in fields or hoe
The garden, calling out for Papa verses
We'd have to say that week in Sunday school,
Our voices tangling in the wind. *My days*
Are swifter than a weaver's shuttle ... And I
Will dwell in the house of the Lord ... We shall
Not all sleep, but we shall all be changed.
Then when I saw the sun begin to fall
And all our shadows disappearing in dusk,
Sister and I would leave to clean and fill
The coal-oil lamps, rubbing with soft cloths
Until the darkness of the night before was gone
And globes shone clear as mirrors, lit and glowing

To let the others know that it was time
To come inside and rest.
                    On Saturdays
And sometimes summer evenings, to pay our duns,
We combed the countryside for windpicked bones
And bits of broken glass, sky-filled skulls
And scraps of metal, any tossed-off thing
To sell the salvage yard in Sweetwater.
Sundays we spent almost all day in church.
And every summer we would work real hard
So we could lay the fields by a week and drive
Each day to hear some wide-lapelled, wide-jowled
Revival preacher pour into the air
A lake of fire, the unforgiven souls
Burning in it, their cries still clear to me
Long after everyone was saved. Those nights
I couldn't close my eyes; I'd lie quiet
Until my trembling, like a breeze so slight
It seems a secret passed from leaf to leaf,
Entered Sister too. When Mama came
To say goodnight and found us sitting up
In bed or holding hands beneath the sheets,
She stayed, the cornshuck mattress rustling us
Together and her childhood rising as
We settled, names and faces in the air
Like sudden shapes in clouds you don't quite see
When someone points to them, or see
Just as they drift apart. But sometimes, warm
Toward sleep, when Mama's voice was like a voice
Muted through walls, I'd feel my hands go cold

Against the only pane of light for miles,
And see, inside, a woman and a child,
Grandma Boatwright and Mama, late at night,
Piecing the very quilt that covered me.
Or I would pause in the leaf-sifted light
Beyond her secret clearing in the trees,
Because a branch cracked underfoot, or the dead
Leaves whispered where I was, and Mama, lost
In thought, a child, had lifted up her head
And looked right through me, listening ...

I knew,

Though it was years before she said a word
About it, Mama wanted to leave. Once,
While Papa blessed our food and prayed the day
Might come we'd own that farm, she squeezed my hand
Until it hurt and kept on squeezing hard
A moment when the prayer was done, let go
Finally and looked in Papa's eyes and said
Amen. She'd keep a letter from Carolina
A week or more, before she'd bring it out
One night when everyone was on the porch
And read into the evening's scattered sounds,
Her voice at times so soft it seemed to change
Into a killdeer's cry, carrying far
Across the fields and coming back as words
Again: details and conversations which,
Later, when I would read the letters myself,
Weren't there. And she would always try to lead
Grandma or Grandpa back into that world
With her, asking questions and unraveling

Answers until they'd start remembering too,
Their lives like smoke unspooling from a candle's
Flame, lazily curling into the air
Until the years they'd lived had melted down
To that particular moment: Mama folding up
The letter, no one making a sound, and the fireflies
Flashing out in the dark yard like keyholes
From moving rooms.

                  Grandma died one day
Inside the wellhouse, or didn't die right then,
Perhaps, but went away. The week she lay
In the hospital at Roscoe, even when her tongue
Would nudge her lip for snuff that wasn't there,
Or when some ruined word escaped
Into the air above her, and Grandpa leaned
Down close repeating softly, *Here, here now,*
I knew she wasn't there. Sister had found her;
Then Cole had found them both, Sister kneeling
Amid the shattered pitcher Grandma had filled,
In the fading shadow spilled into the dirt
Around her, tearlessly whispering her name,
Smoothing her hair.

                 I never went in there
Again without remembering her, small things
Usually, sayings and such: *You'll lose a sight
Before you're done. Stop mopin' like a polecat.
The Lord don't give us more than we can bear.*
But once, in the gasp and hush before the pump
Kicked in, when deep within the earth I heard,
Or thought I heard, dark water stir, I closed

My eyes and felt her with me, younger than I
Had ever known her, my age, fourteen, quiet,
Trying to hold in all the life that teemed
Inside of her. Before I moved or spoke
The wellhouse turned into a shining room
Where she was working, older, through a cloud
Of flour smiling surprise at seeing me,
Her apron dusted with faint shapes of hands
Like prints of ghosts. Spreading her arms out wide,
She faded, or didn't fade so much as change,
Emerge into my memory of her, aging
Into the moment just before she fell:
The pitcher in her hands unbroken, water
Pouring into it, her eyes bewildered, pleading ...
The spigot shuddered off: I was alone.
Sunlight riddled the wooden roof and walls,
The dust suspended in it, weightless, shifting,
And the water I was holding so cold and clear
It seemed, with that first trembling sip, to fill
My throat with light.
                                    Grandpa lived three more years,
But wandered from our lives and from his own.
Most nights, right up until he died, he walked
The broken road between our house and town
To sit on the wildflowered ground among a clutch
Of graves, the moon-cool stones and crosses sprouting
In an unclaimed and fenceless field. In bed,
Drifting, I'd hear sometimes his late returnings,
The silent house unsettling, footsteps, mutterings,
A door touched softly shut. But early once,

A morning when the fields were lost in mist
And quietly one by one we'd filed outside,
We found him standing in the gauzed dawn,
His face fevered and pearled, his eyes alive
With something he was dying to say.
                                        We kept
Their things, and no one moved into their room
Or even mentioned doing so. There was a change
You felt the moment you had stepped inside,
A pulsing silence like the wake of bells,
Some space in things you had to always move
Carefully around to keep from falling into:
The razor strop that Grandpa used to wave
Above him, laughing and lamenting
He hadn't used it more on Papa, Grandma's
Honest snuffbox, a yellow shaving mug,
A little softwood cross that Papa couldn't
Remember carving as a child. One day,
I watched him lift it from the windowsill,
Staring at fields he'd worked all morning in:
The plow abandoned, a row half-plowed, the day's
Slow waves of heat rising.
                              It seemed our lives
Had quickened then. The boys were never home,
And Papa plowed by moonlight, came in nights
Too tired to eat. One day I found a box
Of sheets and pillowslips that Mama said
She'd made for me to use when I was gone.
I guess I hadn't thought of being gone.
But like a dream that every night returns,

Or like the music to a song whose words
You don't know, some rhythm lingering,
That moment in her room became a place
Where every day I wandered, smoothing cool
Sheets on a bed, unclouding mirrors, arranging
And rearranging rooms I'd never seen.
But then I'd breathe the warm reek of stalls,
A sudden gust of sun-soured clabber, feel
The washpot's haze of heat, a needle's prick,
Or hear, from under eaves or in a slowly
Lightening field, one dove haunting the dawn ...
And I was back, humming something, at work
Around that farm I knew so well — from the least
Creak of a door or board to all the hiding
Places in the maize — I could have closed
My eyes, or risen any moonless night,
And walked remembering in the dark.

III

A drought descended like a fever then.
For a long time no one would say the word,
Though you could feel at dawn the rainless days
Deep in the ground like sunlight in a stone,
The breeze a breath that's gently blown on kindling.
Then it didn't matter. The sun screamed heat.
Buds withered inward. Day by day the fields,
Rootless and ruined, thin as siftings, drifted —
Until the wind blew hard, a sandstorm swirled
Away the sun, and the whole house ached
And sang. Inside that sound, in lighted rooms,
We watched damp cheesecloth screens across the windows
Darken, discovered grit between our sheets
And in the icebox, and even in our sleep
We tasted dust. Papa went halfway mad.
God came into his brain like water poured
Into a wasp nest, and he called even coffee sin.
Cole and Joe took off to California. M.A.
Married his schoolteacher, Opal (scant
Two years before I married mine).

                                    Opal's eyes
Were all horizon. Looking in, you knew
That what you saw was your own vision's limit,
And not the end of what was there. In prayers,
She'd catch you looking up and wink. She'd cry
At any little kindness, if you just said
You thought her face was pretty, or the time
We saw Sister giving her only piece

Of candy to the mare. Once, when the drought
Had ended and a gullywashing rain
Lashed panes and simmered in the flooded fields,
M.A. was gone an hour or more in search
Of her. When they came in, I went for towels
And offered one to Opal: dripping, shining,
So happy she scared me. She paused, said my name
Like a soft promise.
                                        Opal told me once
That if you closed your eyes and saw his face
Clearly, and if when you were with him time
Went by like water through your hands, you knew
You were in love; and when I walked that fall
Into eleventh grade and first saw Tom —
Sunburnt, the tiny lines he squinted smiling,
His white shirt ironed all wrong — it seemed his eyes
Were eyes that I'd been dreaming, and I heard,
Through all the voices and the settling in,
Like drops of water dripping into water,
The small desk clock ticking. Tom heard it too.
Not halfway through that class he paused and looked
Outside and asked some easy, long-forgotten
Question of me, a space around each word
As if there were some secret meaning in it.
I let the silence settle on the class.
I waited while a hand or two went up
In the air —Tom turning half around, the sunstruck
Schoolbell on his desk so bright it seemed almost
Sound — then looked up right into his eyes
And answered.

Almost eighteen months went by
Before the school board ever knew a thing.
We'd meet down by the creek on Saturdays,
Or Tom would come for dinner after church
And spend all afternoon and evening with us
On the farm. Some nights, when Papa fell asleep
Out on the porch, and Mama when I asked
Looked long and hard at Tom and slowly nodded,
We took Tom's car and over the washboard roads
Rattled laughing clear across the county
To lie out in the open while the stars
Came out, recalling from another night
The life that lay somewhere ahead of us:
How Tom would be a preacher like his papa,
And we would have a family and a farm;
How in some far-off dark we'd lie awake
And talk as we were talking then, and the names
That we were saying into stars would be
Our children sleeping, the moments flowing by
Would be a stillness we would understand.
And though those earliest nights together,
When side by side we stared into the space
Unending over and the starlight sleeked
Our skin, we hardly touched — my fingers lingering
Along his throat to feel his pulse, a kiss
So feathery it might have been the wind
That brushed my cheek— I felt that chance existing
In the air, I felt the years desiring us,
Drawing us in.
          Tom's Papa married us

In April in our yard. The next few years,
Though we were hardly scraping by, I wished
For nothing at all; or wishes came like sounds
In sleep, were mine before I knew I'd made them.
Light cleared the kitchen windowpane and changed
My face into the fields of our small farm
Just north of Roscoe, where the songs of birds
Became the birds, rising out of the leaves,
And Tom, bare-shouldered in his overalls,
Waved as he walked out of the dawn toward me.
Light gleamed later from clean white shirts hung smooth
As envelopes; the fresh-turned garden steamed.
Preserves were cooled and sealed in Mason jars
And were the long hard hours of work I'd done,
Gradually learning to let the wind that cried
From out of the fields or pried unlatched doors
Be wind, the grasping shadows only shadows,
The slowly falling sun a sign that Tom
Was almost home. I learned to cook and drive
A car, a piece of eggshell boiled in coffee
Keeps acid down, you always test an iron
On shirttails first, smooth cuffs and collars stiff
As canning wax. I learned to be alone.
And every evening for a month or more,
In summer, as we tore the mouldered porch
Away and built another, board by board —
The birds becoming only sounds again,
The light like steeping tea — I learned to sand
The ends, to keep a saw from quivering,
To hammer every piece into its place

And then to lean eye-level with a level
To see that it was true.
                                  Sometimes M.A.,
Before the sun untangled from the gnarled
Mesquite tree in our yard, came by to say
That Opal had the sulls and could I stay
A spell with her and help take care of Roland.
One winter morning, in a chiselling wind,
I found her standing in frost-blistered fields,
Her nightgown whipping like a wisp of cloud
Clinging to her. I called and called. I came
So close our breaths mingled in the air, her face
As white as ice and just as still. And once,
When I'd walked calling through the dawning house,
Found Roland sleeping peaceful in his crib
And gone all tight inside, quiet now,
I looked into an unlit room and all
I saw were eyes, blazing out of nowhere,
Unwavering, as if it were the darkness
Watching me.
                        But all the other times
I showed up early there, she'd laugh out loud
And swear my hair looked like a tumbleweed
And that she'd never begin to understand
How she could love so utterly a man
No smarter than a mule, then toss a rag
Or wave me toward the kitchen to help with chores.
I loved the way she dreamed up things for Roland,
The way her hands could ease his cries to silence,
Or understand what silence shined to say.

A thimble was a junebug's hat, or a bell
Only a bird could hear; her needle dipped,
Stopped, and then flashed back answers to the sun.
A place where he had fallen was a place
Where the world needed to be touched, and tears,
When she had kissed that pain away, were seeds
They planted in the ground. She told him once
The little roly-polies under rocks
Were baby rocks, a worm was living mud.
The windmill was a clock, she said (squinting
Through wind), and it was almost time to sleep.
While Roland napped, and while the shadows crept
Across the floor, we talked, Opal at the old
Piano, though like as not she'd leave the keys
Untouched, her hands just lightly resting there.
But sometimes, suddenly, as if her words
Had turned to music and the music meant
Just what she'd wanted to say, she'd leave off talking
And start to play, softly, until it seemed
I hardly heard a sound at all — drifting
Listening — the notes like snow that falls at night,
Covering quiet houses, over known roads
And fields, and to the limbs of leafless trees
Clinging, until you wake into a world
That's lost its edges.
                    It seemed those seasons swirled
Into each other, as if icicles dripped
An April rain, or a blown dandelion
Became the snow. In unsown, dew-sharpened fields
I'd blink and be — a glittering instant — stilled

In the smells and shimmery whispers of the ripe
And only crop of wheat we ever grew.
In nights so cold our breaths plumed the hard dark
Above our bed, I thought of white, taut,
Rain-laden clouds and felt, as we grew warm
Together under quilts, the long shudders
Of summer thunder.
                          I knew, without a doubt,
The night I first got pregnant; just as I knew,
Shivering out of sleep three months away,
Unpeeling sodden sheets and waking Tom,
That child was gone. Because the doctor said
I'd worked too hard, next time I went to bed,
Watched broomweed thriving in our garden, dust
In the house so thick that Tom would leave *I love you*
Scrawled on a countertop or windowpane.
But in the night that child was taken too.
Each time I thought I couldn't make it. Each time,
For weeks, remembering, I'd go cold all over,
Burning the way you burn when you first plunge
Into some freezing pool, gasping, quickened —
Until in time the water warms to you,
And you can move unfeeling through it. All told,
In seven years, I had four children die
Inside of me. I've twice delivered silence.
When my one son came crying free of me,
I closed my eyes and praised God. I praised the pain.
Over and over in that humid room
I breathed his name.
                          By then, the War was on,

Tom was gone, so I moved back home
To Champion and the room that all those years
I'd shared with Sister, hung my clothes on nails
In the walls again and cradled David all
Night long under Grandma Boatwright's quilt,
As if it were my touch that kept him breathing.
Those first few weeks, when he just slept and ate —
Head-heavy as a sunflower, his motions slow
As someone underwater — I spent whole days
Just watching him: his eyes becoming blue
As Tom's, his face uncrumpling into mine.
I went ten months without a single letter,
Then got an armload all at once and passed
An afternoon untangling dateless days
Down by the teeming creek, piecing places
Where I could see him as he sounded, aged,
Changed, some real world from which he might return.
I wrote a letter almost every day,
Traced David's hands out on a page sometimes
So Tom would know how big he was. Later,
I wrote down words and where he'd learned them. *Rain*
In the rain; *moon* one night in Mama's arms.
I always swore and still am almost sure
He first said *Mama* in his sleep. And once, late,
When hand in hand we'd walked beyond the yard,
Where in the shifting breeze the leaves of cotton
Moved, touched, then settled back until it seemed
Whole fields were gently tilting like the slow
Heave of a sea, he said, softly, echoing me,
Field, field, field, field.

Tom never talked
About that time we were apart, except
To say, when nearly thirty years had passed
And in the darkness we were watching words
We knew by heart becoming always only ours —
Our letters burning, the night air starred with sparks —
I'd live it all again, to know such love.
He never mentioned preaching either. God
Was in the past. Or God was in the dry
Unyielding fields which for eleven years
After the War was over, sun to sun,
Tom studied like a book. Or in the wide,
Excited eyes of little David, who,
Until that day we met the train in Dallas,
Tom hadn't ever even seen. Careful,
Mumbling, he lifted David in his arms,
Showed him the close ocean inside the shell
He'd brought him, whirling inward like an ear.
When I came close and touched my lips to Tom's,
I could taste his tears.
                        We bought a farm
Nine miles from Snyder, near the locker plant,
And with a rush of restless labor claimed
The place: the house in order, a garden started,
Across the tilled and seeded fields tendrils
Like green fingers reaching out of the earth.
It wasn't long before I knew each nick
And scuff by touch in the cellar's cold stone walls,
Knew all the unsafe places in the yard
Where David couldn't play. I could drive blind

The road between our house and Opal's, or all
The way to Champion, where on Saturdays
I did our wash in Mama's new machine,
Then cooked or cleaned while Opal tended hers.
Late those days, when the men came in from fields,
We'd have an evening meal together. Then,
Provided the night was nice, we dragged our chairs
Out in the yard and while the long day drained
From our faces and shadows piled in drifts,
Absorbing shapes of things, we talked, Tom
Relaxing as he hardly ever did,
And even Papa eased. But there was something,
Those nights, that kept me mostly quiet. Something,
When rasping in the air a flame appeared
And wavered over M.A.'s pipe, made me strain
To see each person sitting in their place;
To hear, when everyone was laughing loud
Or all the locusts in the fields and trees
Shrilled like a great big ratchet tightening,
The voices of the children as they played
In darkness. There was something not yet passed,
In the calm, undone, ours, I could feel it.
As on a summer night sometimes you feel
Heat-lightning when the sky's completely dark,
A shimmering in the air that grows and grows,
Flaring in a sudden soundless sheet of light
That for one moment lets you see the world—
A windmill stilled out in a field, a face
Like shadowed brass, upturned, familiar, near —
And then that moment's gone.

                                 There were quick shouts
And laughter: Sister chasing David outside.
There was a fire burning under the washpot,
Rippling the air, the copper bottom glowing,
Water hot for Opal when she came. Light,
Above the loaded stove, quivered color
Through beads of steam that on the underside
Of cabinets formed, and hung, and did not fall.
And Mama — I remember — moulding bread dough
In loaf pans, when the car came skidding up,
Stopped, breathed in deep, the moist dough slowly closing
Where her hands had been. Before I reached the door
I heard one sound repeated softly like
A question I might pause and understand,
The way you wait above wind-shaken water
For the face you see to be your own. The sun
Slammed against the chrome and dazzled back
Into the heat-bleared air. And then I heard
Quite clearly — *Opal, Opal* — as M.A. leaned
And lifted, like a sack of goods that water
Has soaked all through, the slumped and bloody shape
Of Opal, spilling out of herself
Into his arms.
                    Tom said I passed whole days
In silence. Other times, he'd say my name
And I would only say it back to him,
Over and over, fading, like a well
Repeating sound until that sound is gone.
He said one night I squeezed his arm so hard
I left faint bruises there; that once, at Champion,

They found me talking to myself inside
The wellhouse, eyes shut tight as early bolls.
All I remember are pieces of dreams:
The farthest reaches of a porch's crawlspace,
Trapped air, dust in my lungs, legs tingling sleep:
My shadowed family kneeling one by one
In the yawn of sun, looking in. Plowed fields
At dawn, the broken acres breathing, clouds
Revealing in rifts and slow healings wind
I could not feel. Voices, a yard at night,
A firefly touched too hard, a little dust
Of light no longer life in my hands.
And Opal, always Opal: with a gun
Appearing, in tears, in a doorway saying
M.A., honey, if you don't want to see this ...
Then down the worn path winding past the barn
At Champion as the sun was falling I
Was running, into the fields and faster now,
Feeling the cotton changing into maize,
Across the dried-up creek, wide grazing land
And all the way to the edge of what was ours:
The river where the trees grew green along
The bank and the scissortails sheared the air;
And where my line was taut and swerving once,
In summer, silt billowing through the water
And pain like brightly colored scarves unfurling
In my arms and Grandpa rushing through the grass
Behind me shouting *Hold on, Josie, hold on!*

IV

Down in the cellar where our small light died
In nooks and in the air beyond us — steps
Ascending out of sight, the far walls gone —
We heard the first hard gust, a long crack
And wake of quiet, like a bolt of cloth
Torn clean in two. Tom whispered something lost.
I watched the lamp's flame dance in David's eyes,
Squeezed his hand gently once as he squeezed mine.
Then somewhere in the darkness over us
The tied-down door began to buck and whine
As wind came slivering in. I dreamed a cloud
Raveled and black and scrawling on the ground
And what it touched was taken in: a tree
Uprooted tumbling through the air, a house
Like matchwood snapped and scattered. It lasted hours,
Or it seemed hours, for all through that storm
That blasted half the county's crops and killed
A woman wandering in the fields, they said,
To see, I hardly moved, I didn't speak
A word. Then when the storm was over, and the rain
That followed, nailing down the far-off door,
Was long over, we climbed the stone-stepped throat
Into what light there was — bone light, moonlight —
To find the house intact, our tree half-sheared
But there, through its thinned shock of limbs the wind
Soft in the spared leaves.
                    That was June —
Thistle and beargrass, if alive, in bloom.

That was the summer when one Sunday Tom,
Suited, clean-shaven in the rain-woven dawn,
Was at a window when I woke, his eyes
Uneasy as he reached for me, his sun-
Soaked face wrung white. He held me hard. Light drops
Pricked light across the puddles in the yard.
Tom went to church with us again, and sang
A little louder every week, his voice
Untangling as the words returned; David's
Changing, one moment deeper than the days
He'd known, then striking high with what was left
Of childhood in him. It was afterwards,
Milling in the aisles, that I first heard
They wanted Tom to be the principal
At Snyder. I remember driving home:
Fields, clouds, the quiet miles. And it was weeks
Away, another blazing day when Tom
Stormed angry early from our sandy fields
Complaining that his back was dealing fits,
Or saying hallelujah we were here,
The promised land, eternity, such
Abundance and a sun that never sets —
I cooled a rag in water, and from the burn
Above his collar, his cheeks, each tiny line
Around his eyes, I wiped the fields away;
Then answered what he could not bring himself
To ask me.
          Although I wandered all through
The truck and plunder of our unpacked boxes,
And even drove alone before the farm

Was sold to comb the rooms, the empty barn,
The cold, root-walled cellar, it must have been,
I must have known, that those few things I thought
I'd lost while we were moving had been lost
Before but never noticed, like a song
You would have sworn you knew until in church
One day it's rising, changing, going on
Without you ...

                    Tom was easier than I'd seen
In years. He used his paddle sparingly,
And though it would have been incredible
To those he caught, when he woke gifted once
With a sweet-reeking cloud inside his car,
A polecat nosing at the rolled-up glass,
He laughed. He'd come home calm from brittle meetings,
Sit patiently through sleeting football games
Where he knew everyone and everyone
Kept interrupting as I tried to find,
Emerging from the crush of mud and limbs,
The mud and uncrushed limbs of David. Clean,
Half-drowsing over supper, David ate
Then turned in early every Thursday night,
Tossing and talking softly in his sleep,
Life working in him like a secret
He could not keep. I touched his dreaming face,
Then turned away. I'd stay up half the night
Arranging, rearranging, going one
More time through the pictures that Mama gave me,
Grainy, faded, like old wood shot with light:
Grandma and Grandpa; Mama young and dressed

In white; Papa in the open, squinting hard;
The boys; Sister; the river where a line
Of saved were wading in, too far and blurred
To tell which one was me.
                                    I woke alone.
The sheets were cold as I rolled slowly over,
Sleep tugging at me like the tingling reaches
Of water when you break back into air,
Now moving constantly to keep yourself
There. In the cool hours, past the walnut's shade,
I hoed tall weeds and scrabbled out caliche,
Wheelbarrowed topsoil and buried seeds.
Two rooms I painted; pictures stilled the hall.
Into the washer's rackety dance at ten
The mailman clicked up steps, stopped, clicked away.
An engine idled in the vacuum's whine:
Tom was home at noon. Nearby church bells chimed
At two, three, four, until the hours were matched
And sorted like a batch of folded clothes.
I put them all still warm away. I made,
Out of the ticking sameness of a day,
Another block to piece into the quilt
Of clothes that David kept outgrowing, rooms
That gleamed and gradually came to mind
Whenever someone asked me where I lived,
And a meal that every evening, straight at six,
Steamed in our praying faces. Supper done,
David spread out his homework in front of Tom.
And in that mix of maps and grammar, names,
Dates, numbers tumbling into something known,

I did the dishes, staring out the window
At tendrils, rained-on furrows, ruined blooms,
Icicles, honeysuckle, laden stalks
And late vines locked in frost, a black trunk burled
Like a half-melted candle, four o'clocks
Splayed wide at dusk ...
                      While Papa was alive —
Before the pain that by the time he'd told us,
Tearless, had carved a year inside of him
Paused finally when he was sitting in the sun,
Then eased, his cedar rocker creaking down
To quiet like a treelimb in the wind
As the wind moves on — we drove on Saturdays
To Champion as we always had, and worked,
And ate an evening meal, and under the tall
Pecan tree rested while the locusts' whine
Tightened and the last light glowed in the bones
Of leaves. Most afternoons a little while
I'd take a walk around the farm with David;
And Papa, if he saw us, followed, light
And silent, holding my shoulder as we crossed
The fields, as if in any sudden gust
He might rise. Moments opened everywhere.
Out of the trickling creek we stepped in stride
Rushed days of rain from deep in David's childhood
(A roar I caught him crawling toward in time),
Which drained away into the jigsawed bed
Of mine: dust and brush from which I climbed slow
And dignified when Mozelle Bratcher, cockleburred,
Crying, apologized because she'd called

My family trash. Grandma watched it all,
Plucked healing weed, stuck chewed-up beet leaves
On nicks and cuts, and never breathed a word.
By then, almost any story I started
David could finish for me, recalling cures
I'd made him take, lukewarm corn-silk tea,
Onion eaten until he'd cried away
Some pain, reminding me of rain that soaked
The road and mired the undertaker's tires
In mud the morning Grandpa, dreamless, stayed
In bed. *God's finger touched him,* Papa said,
And he slept.
                    Mama left the farm to us
And moved with Sister back to Carolina.
We hired a man to see to things, the hens
And such, but when in June we drove to spend
The summer, Tom and I, alone, we found
A bullsnake curled in a cool, uncovered churn,
Weevils teeming in the untended cotton.
Days passed before in brush and waist-high grass
I stumbled sticky from the fog of rot
Our missing mare — sun-rummaged, gauzed in flies —
Was lifting into. It was all at first
Half-wasted labor, quick, unthinking work,
The way you whittle, Papa told me, blind
A while until you find the shape wood needs
To be. In sunlight sun-plucked fencewire flashed
And vanished. Dawn flared on a fire-scarred field.
Each night between the clouded sounds of cowbells,
That distant broken music I had heard,

Half-heard, as long as I remembered, silence
Widened. By August, when the sharp blade slipped
Through sheetrock I was slicing and I felt
My legs go hollow and my whole body cold —
Words tumbling from me, blood flowering down the wall —
There wasn't much left to do at all. That night,
All night, Tom held me in his arms. I stole
Away before the sun was up, to the porch,
To stand there looking into what I knew
Were fields, the windmill creaking in the breeze,
The wellhouse and the henhouse, limbs and leaves
Somewhere in the air above the yard,
Where though no part of the darkness answered
One bird kept calling and calling.

                                The cows were gone.
The hens, the fields but for the burned-off closest —
Two acres like an island in the wide
Wind-riffled whiteness someone farmed, it seemed,
From farther and farther away — were gone. The blood
Was painted over and my stitched-up hand
Was nearly healed when Mama, home for good,
Walked out into the yard. And though her voice
Had hardly wavered when she'd left before;
Though in the long black line that filed by Papa
(Clean-suited, laid out with clasped hands, caulked pores)
She had paused, tearless touched the smooth-stone coolness,
Then walked on, in the yard that day, in wind
That whipped her blue best dress and swayed her shadow
Fast on the grass like shadowed flames, she cried,
And spoke to no one though I held her close:

Not a cloud in the sky.
                         David spent
That summer selling Bibles on the road.
At first, whenever he was passing by,
He'd stop to practice on us, blunt and fumbling
Thick-fingered in the wispy pages. Soon,
When he stepped booming from his car and plied,
Tom muttered, Scripture like a pack of cards,
We knew he hadn't sold enough. Tom stood,
Stalled, pondered weather or the cost of feed,
Or told him as he took his suited arm
And guided him out toward the reeking barn
That too much reading was a weariness
To the flesh. I remember everything
About the only evening David stayed.
I made a meal for ten, and on the porch
Just after, talk and laughter trailing off,
I saw the heartwood swirl of sunset hold
Together long enough to be alive,
A deer maybe, when even as I spoke
Melted back into the seething evening,
So brief I wasn't sure just where it was,
Or if it was. David paced and planned, always
Almost elsewhere, already spending years
That he was saving for. I still can hear
His voice that night explaining where he'd live
Come fall in Abilene, that trailer house
Where Mama — after Tom had towed it home,
And Sister got a job and place to stay
In Loraine — lived for over eighteen years

In our back yard, weaving her life so tight
With mine that by the time her memories thinned
At the scattered last like a long kept letter
Through which in folds and creases you begin
To see, she'd call most nights to ask me something:
What was she wearing when she first met Papa?
What did we leave behind in Carolina?
Now where was little David living? Why?
She let her breath out slowly when I told her,
Turned off the light that through her window cast
A window on the grass, and never said
Goodbye.
        After Tom's first heart attack,
After his leg had swollen slowly black,
Clotted, burned by a cold and smokeless fire,
I lived listening. Dropped change, a wincing hinge,
A floorboard warping like a cry of pain —
And I would rush to find Tom rolling dimes
For savings, piddling with his fishing gear,
Or wavering caneless as he learned to walk
Again, his arms stretched out wide, balancing,
As if on either side there was some space
That only he could see. Some nights, when some
Late-settling bird unsettled me, and Tom
Lay moonskinned, moving slightly, skimming dreams,
I'd nudge him till he grumbled. Then one dawn
I woke and he was still in bed beside me,
Unbreathing, sleeping deeper than my voice
Could reach. I leaned down close, almost believing —
Until I saw cracks and a silly trembling

Like a chick-pecked egg as he smiled alive
And kissed me quickly. Even after Tom
Was back at work and every afternoon
Walked home, I was alert and nervous, words
Quicksilvery when I tried to tell him why,
One more time, I was calling. So many hours
I couldn't fill, stillnesses I could feel
Too well: Tom's polished schoolbell on the shelf;
Clouds curdling toward a storm; the telephone
I rushed inside to answer, no one there,
The air ringing and ringing when the screen door
Slammed the empty house around me.
                                        Sometimes —
That Sunday David married Fran; or when Tom
One summer gathered tools more sun than wood
And painted everything one evening red —
It seemed I'd gone to sleep and woke up older.
No. I was so careful. But the years
Grew quiet, and I moved quietly through them:
As in a field of scrub mesquite and brush
Where you know quail are nesting your mind wanders,
You misstep, and the ground around you turns
To birds: a sudden rush of wings and cries
Receding, and the hard beating of your heart
As all at once you watch them go. *Speak now,*
The preacher told us, *or forever hold*
Your peace. Tom turned, his white shirt wiped with paint
And rust like finger-streaks of dusk, stood
So odds and ends were in the picture too:
A broken hoe, heel-bolts and clevises,

The yoke and coulter of a moldboard plow.
Now, Tom said, smiling wide, his deep-creased face
Like ground in drought, or tiny rivers
Turning into one.

                Even as our tires
Hummed on the paving and the hint of light
Eased from the level ground before the dawn,
Graining the air, I was still asking Tom
Please don't go. Darkness dwindled into phonewires,
Pumpjacks, the cricks and knots of bare mesquites;
Crows flecked off, flying low across the fields.
It was an easy hour, Tom said, his hand
Tightening on mine, the cotton gin, the sign
For highway 10, the schoolhouse and the church
Emerging just as I remembered, roads
Unraveling home. At Champion, while the sun
Pulled all its bloodshot colors into one,
And brightened, and the yard's dry, brittle weeds,
Waist-high in places, blazed and wilted black
As they passed a small fire on, Tom kept
Reminding me to move away from him,
Kept moving faster as unsmothered flames,
Like living things, flicked past the tilted piece
Of plywood he let fall, lifted, let fall.
We were so close. The house wavered in the haze.
Smoke frayed and faded as it rose. Sweat spread
Like shadows through Tom's shirt. The doctor said
Tom likely died before he hit the ground,
And never felt the fire that scorched one side
Before I dragged him clear, the searing smoke

Night after night I woke up choking through
With nothing in my hands. Let it be true.
Flames slashed and flourished in the last tall weeds
Seething toward fields and toward the porch, heat
Warping over the blown glass of the air.
Then I could hear, everywhere, fire, the spit
And crack as old wood quick as kindling caught,
Steps and chairs, doors, walls, windows shattering
And sirens wailing in that shining time
I can't remember clearly, can't forget —
Before a man leaned from the melting light
Alive, and real hands reached out of the heat
Into my hiding place I could not leave:
Still rubbing at the darkness on Tom's face
And feeling for his breathing as I tried
To give him mine and holding on to hear
One more time that last whisper that the doctor,
Gently, said I had likely never heard.

Josie   Josie

Let it, dear God, be true.
                              David stayed
A month with me, and sometime in that drowse
Of visits, whispers, flowers, sold the farm
Because, he said, I told him to. Days
Stabbed past blinds, missing; in the barbed dark,
I lay wide-eyed fighting sleep. Mama cooked, cleaned,
Cried quietly for me as, sorting Tom's things,
I tried to smooth a wrinkled shirt, lingered

Over stray coins or keys, the tiny diary
I'd never known Tom kept the first eight months
That he was overseas. A week was blank
When there was nothing worth remembering. Waves,
Late, gently rocked the water where he lay,
Cradled awake, thinking of me. Words
One day all ran together and I read:
This is happening in the lightest rain.
Day by day, room by room, in the yard, the shed,
I had to touch it all, each thing of Tom's —
Even the bait-filled battered cattle trough
Behind the trailer; even the fish Tom caught
Just days before he died; until in time,
Tears finally mine, I let it mostly go.
Worms curled into the garden's turned-up soil
Like moving roots. Small, frozen hard, the fish
Tom kept because I'd doubted fish were there
Flashed in the night air over Towle Park Pond,
Sinking deep into dreams, little quivers
Of light quickening to their first world,
Shining far from me like a shattered moon,
Not to be caught again ever.

                          Opal told me once,
Out of the blue, that she would live, it seemed,
Through anything. She said some mornings came
And she was not quite in them, not alive
Enough to lift a hand when Roland's cry
From right beside her spiralled out of a well,
Or M.A., leaving, leaning down to kiss her,
Whispered slivers of glass. She said she'd walked

Out in the blistered fields that winter day
To feel the slow chill moving through her, ice,
Fingers freezing half-broken in the cold.
To feel. You wake and you sleep, she said, sleep
And wake, until there's nothing to hold on to,
Nothing. She said the worst pain's knowing pain
Will pass.
          Tom's face grew fainter every day.
His eyes were everywhere: the gas jet's flame,
A jay's quick wing, my irises in bloom,
The cool, blue fractures of the daylight moon.
I watched the tall tree greening and the time
Slipped by, light widening in the fallen leaves.
I watched the clouds that drifted in the clear sky
Float broken sifting through the leafless limbs,
Over the ruined garden and the yard,
The windowsill, as snow. I felt afraid.
That night, long after Mama's light was out,
And jagged down my body and the walls
The shadows of the fire were raveled back
Into the grate — a log of intact ash,
One ember's innards like a shining hive —
I couldn't for the life of me be still.
Coatless, thoughtless, I left the house and drove
Alone into the countryside, not knowing
But knowing not to wonder where I was going
Or why. Past straggled farms, down market roads
And even unpaved roads, I turned and turned,
My headlights jolting over quilted fields
And back again, until no windows glowed

From distant houses and there were no cars
As far as I could see. Then I left mine.
Out in the cat-tongued wind, cold needling in,
I sank up to my ankles in the snow
Plunging half-stumbling into unfenced fields
Farther and farther, breathing harder, sharp air,
Nowhere, no one behind me when I stopped.
My white breath bloomed and faded, bloomed and slowed.
The quiet clenched around me. Nothing stirred.
Clabber, clear water, killdeer, closed bolls
Yawning cotton, dawn-threaded locust skins
And dew-soothed faces peaceful in their sleep:
I thought of Tom, of high, unheaded maize ...
And I turned, dream-fingers linked with mine to lead
Me home, the way I'd taken like a seam
Laid out between the unsown fields of darkness.

V

My grandson walks through walls he does not see.
Touching nothing, he touches tools and stalls,
A bucket and a clutch of warm eggs:
The torn-down henhouse, wellhouse and the barn.
He wonders where the fenceline was, the maize,
The garden and the yard; stands blinking back
The brightness under the unshadowing eaves
Of the house, even the shade tree sheared away,
High cotton blooming in these rooms of air.
My grandson, leaning over the white rows,
Over the long porch gone to light, picks
A lock of cotton and he wants to know
If I would live it all again ...
                                    Wind stirs
In the leaves, in the windmill's vacant blades,
Spinning and spinning without sound. Wind threads
Unwhistling through the windsplit wood, over
The filled-in well where something of the cold
Stone walls, of buried air, clear water, rose
When children we called down to hear a sound
Survive us; and it stirs before it dies
These leaves that rise and fall like the leaves of the tall
Pecan tree in the shadow-flooded yard
When the day was done, the work done, right here,
Where killdeer cried into our silences
And locusts sang themselves out of their skins.

He waits, listening. It is all still now.

for J.C.W. (1915-1995)

75

The Chinese character for poetry is made up of two parts: "word" and "temple." It also serves as pressmark for Copper Canyon Press.

Since 1972, Copper Canyon Press has fostered the work of emerging, established, and world-renowned poets for an expanding audience. The Press thrives with the generous patronage of readers, writers, booksellers, librarians, teachers, students, and funders—everyone who shares the belief that poetry is vital to language and living.

Major funding has been provided by:

Anonymous (2)
The Paul G. Allen Family Foundation
Beroz Ferrell & The Point, LLC
Lannan Foundation
National Endowment for the Arts
Cynthia Lovelace Sears and Frank Buxton
Washington State Arts Commission

For information and catalogs:

COPPER CANYON PRESS
Post Office Box 271
Port Townsend, Washington 98368
360-385-4925
www.coppercanyonpress.org

CPSIA information can be obtained at www.ICGtesting.com
Printed in the USA
LVOW07s1955260816

501819LV00002B/7/P